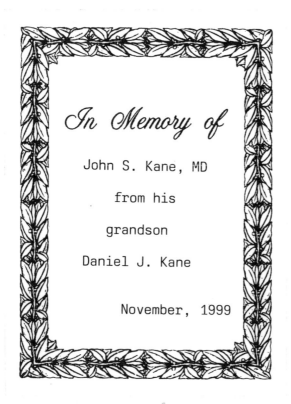

In Memory of

John S. Kane, MD

from his

grandson

Daniel J. Kane

November, 1999

A Note to Parents

Eyewitness Readers is a compelling new program
for beginning readers, designed in conjunction with
leading literacy experts, including Dr. Linda Gambrell,
President of the National Reading Conference and past
board member of the International Reading Association.

Eyewitness has become the most trusted name in
illustrated books, and this new series combines the highly
visual *Eyewitness* approach with engaging, easy-to-read
stories. Each *Eyewitness Reader* is guaranteed to
capture a child's interest while developing his or her
reading skills, general knowledge, and love of reading.

The four levels of *Eyewitness Readers* are aimed
at different reading abilities, enabling you to choose
the books that are exactly right for your children:

Level One – Beginning to read
Level Two – Beginning to read alone
Level Three – Reading alone
Level Four – Proficient readers

The "normal" age at which a child begins to read
can be anywhere from three to eight years old,
so these levels are intended only
as a general guideline.

No matter which level
you select, you can be sure
that you are helping
your child learn to read,
then read to learn!

A DK PUBLISHING BOOK
www.dk.com

Project Editor Penny Smith
Designer Michelle Baxter
Senior Editor Linda Esposito
Managing Art Editor Peter Bailey
US Editor Regina Kahney
Production Josie Alabaster
Picture Research Christine Rista
Natural History Consultant
Colin McCarthy

Reading Consultant
Linda B. Gambrell, Ph.D.

First American Edition, 1998
2 4 6 8 10 9 7 5 3 1
Published in the United States by
DK Publishing, Inc.
95 Madison Avenue, New York, New York 10016

Copyright © 1998 Dorling Kindersley Limited, London

Published in Great Britain by Dorling Kindersley Limited.

Library of Congress Cataloging-in-Publication Data
Dussling, Jennifer.
Slinky, scaly snakes / Jennifer Dussling -- 1st American ed.
p. cm. -- (Eyewitness readers. Level 2)
Summary: An introduction to the physical characteristics
and habits of snakes.
ISBN 0-7894-3439-3 (pbk.) -- ISBN 0-7894-3766-X (hc.)
1. Snakes -- Juvenile literature. [1. Snakes.] I. Title.
II. Series.
QL666.06D87   1998
597.96--dc21
                                98-25068
                                CIP
                                AC

Color reproduction by Colourscan, Singapore
Printed and bound in Belgium by Proost

The publisher would like to thank the following for their
kind permission to reproduce their photographs:
a=above; c=center; b=below/bottom; l=left; r=right; t=top

Bruce Coleman Ltd: Gunter Ziesler 26--27; John Cancalosi
28; John Visser 22, 23t; MPL Fogden 21cl; Rod Williams
16--17; **N.H.P.A.:** Anthony Bannister 24b; Daniel Heuclin
18, 29t; KH Switak 14; **Oxford Scientific Films:** Alastair
Shay 3, 20; **Planet Earth Pictures:** Brian Kenney 12;
Warren Photographic: Jane Burton 9b

EYEWITNESS READERS

BEGINNING TO READ ALONE 2

Slinky, Scaly Snakes!

Written by Jennifer Dussling

DK

DK PUBLISHING, INC.

Slinky, scaly snakes
slide along the ground.

They have legless bodies
and look through unblinking eyes.

Everglades rat snake

Snakes are shiny
and can look slimy.
But they are dry
and smooth to touch.

Rattlesnake

A snake's whole body
is covered in scales.
These scales are hard and tough
like fingernails.

Snakes grow quickly,
but their skin doesn't stretch.
When a snake's skin gets too tight,
the snake has to shed it.
This is called molting.

Rock python

The snake rubs its head
on something rough like a log.
After a few minutes,
the skin begins to peel.

The shed skin of a snake

The snake slides forward
and right out of its skin!
Underneath is a new skin.
It looks bright and shiny.
The snake keeps on growing.
Soon it will be time
to molt again.

Wait and see
When a snake is ready
to molt, its eyes turn
milky white. The snake
is almost blind for a week,
so it stays hidden.

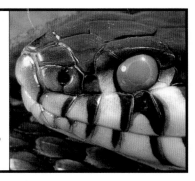

Snakes have no legs.
They move in long, slinky curves.
The ground may look smooth
but it has little bumps everywhere.
A snake pushes off the bumps
to move itself forward.

The sidewinder snake
lives in the desert.
It throws itself forward
one part at a time.
It leaves behind
wavy-looking tracks.

Eyelash viper

Not all snakes live on the ground.
Some live in trees.

Snakes may not have legs,
but they can still climb.
A snake has scales
on its belly
that are larger
than the ones on its back.
These scales grip the tree.
The snake uses
its strong muscles
to pull itself up the tree.

Boa constrictor

How are snakes born?
Some give birth to live babies.
Other snakes lay eggs.

Florida kingsnake laying eggs

Soft shell

Snake eggs
are not hard
like chicken eggs.
The shells are soft,
almost like leather.

A mother snake doesn't usually stay with her eggs.

She lays them in a soft, warm place, then she leaves them.

Soon a baby snake pokes its head out of the egg.

Then it slithers out of its shell.

Rat snake

Haitian (HAY-shun) boa

This snake is not moving.
Only its tongue flicks in and out.
It is checking for danger.

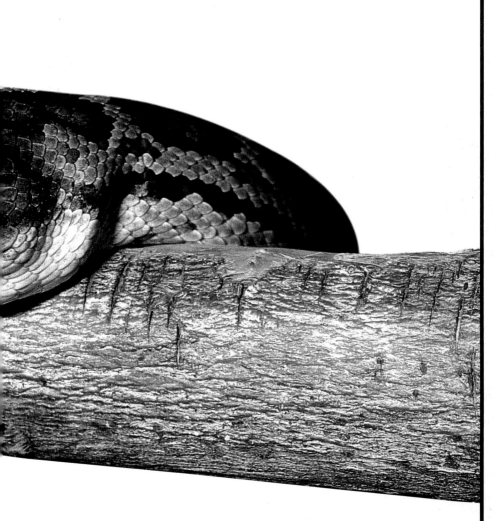

Most snakes can't see or hear well.
But they have
a strong sense of smell.
And they pick up these smells
with their tongues.

A fox meets a whipsnake

But what are snakes afraid of?
Hawks, raccoons, and foxes
like to eat snakes.
Some snakes eat other snakes.
But many snakes have ways
to fool their enemies.

Some snakes blend in
with the area around them.
This vine snake looks like
a vine hanging from a tree.

These gaboon vipers
look like fallen leaves.

Other snakes try to trick
their enemies.

The parrot snake
opens its mouth very wide
and tries to look scary.

The milk snake is harmless.
But it looks like
the deadly coral snake,
so animals stay away.

Coral snake

Milk snake

The grass snake has a great trick.
When an enemy is near,
it plays dead!

All snakes are meat-eaters.
Small snakes eat small animals
like bugs, lizards, and worms.
Some snakes eat eggs.
This snake is swallowing a bird's egg.

Egg-eating snake

The egg makes a big bulge
in the snake's body.

The egg breaks inside the snake.
Then the snake spits out the shell.

A rat makes a tasty meal
for a boa constrictor.

First the snake grabs the rat.
The snake holds on fast
with its strong jaws.

Tight squeeze
Snakes crush their prey,
but they don't break bones.
They squeeze just enough
to make the animal
stop breathing.

It wraps its long body
around and around the rat.
Then the snake starts to squeeze
tight . . . tighter . . . tighter.
Soon the rat's heart stops.

The snake opens its mouth
very, very wide.
It gulps once or twice
and swallows the rat headfirst.

A rock python swallowing a Thomson's gazelle

Big snakes eat bigger animals.
Giant pythons and boas
can be as long as a school bus.
They eat pigs, goats, and gazelles.

Big eaters

A meal can last
a long time.
Snakes like this python
have gone a whole year
without eating!

Mojave rattlesnake

Many snakes use poison
to kill their food.
The poison is stored in sacs
close to their long, sharp fangs.

The snake sticks its fangs
into the animal.

*Uracoan
rattlesnake*

The poison shoots through the
fangs and into the animal's body.
It does not take long
for the animal to die.
Then the snake swallows it whole.

Born to kill
A cobra can kill from
the minute it is born.
Just one tablespoon
of its dried poison
can kill 160,000 mice!

Can snakes hurt people?
Many can.
Here are some snakes
that can poison people.

Rattlesnake

Copperhead

Cobra

But if people are bitten,
snakes can help!
Medicine is made from their poison
to treat snake bites.

Biting people better
A snake bites through
the thin covering
over a container.
Poison dripping from
its fangs is collected.

Snakes are useful in lots of ways.
They eat millions of mice
and other pests.
And they are eaten
by other hungry animals.
Our world would not be the same
without slinky, scaly snakes!

Snake Facts

Snakes are cold-blooded.
They lie in the sun to warm up
and move into the shade
to cool down.

Unlike people,
snakes never stop growing.

The world's heaviest snake
is the anaconda.
It can weigh as much
as three grown men.

The smallest snake
is the thread snake.
It is as skinny
as the lead in a pencil!

Baby snakes have a tooth
to help them break their eggs.
It falls off soon after they hatch.

It's not hard
to outrun a snake.
The fastest ones slither
at the same speed as you walk.

⟦DK⟧ EYEWITNESS READERS

Level 1 *Beginning to Read*
A Day at Greenhill Farm
Truck Trouble
Tale of a Tadpole
Surprise Puppy!
Duckling Days
A Day at Seagull Beach
Whatever the Weather
Busy, Buzzy Bee

Level 2 *Beginning to Read Alone*
Dinosaur Dinners
Fire Fighter!
Bugs! Bugs! Bugs!
Slinky, Scaly Snakes!
Animal Hospital
The Little Ballerina
Munching, Crunching, Sniffing, and Snooping
The Secret Life of Trees

Level 3 *Reading Alone*
Spacebusters
Beastly Tales
Shark Attack!
Titanic
Invaders from Outer Space
Movie Magic
Plants Bite Back!
Time Traveler

Level 4 *Proficient Readers*
Days of the Knights
Volcanoes
Secrets of the Mummies
Pirates!
Horse Heroes
Trojan Horse
Micromonsters
Going for Gold!

Also by Jonathan Galassi

Poetry

MORNING RUN *(1988)*

Translations of Eugenio Montale

THE SECOND LIFE OF ART: SELECTED ESSAYS *(1982)*

OTHERWISE: LAST AND FIRST POEMS *(1984)*

COLLECTED POEMS 1920–1954 *(1998)*

NORTH STREET

NORTH STREET

POEMS BY

JONATHAN

GALASSI

HarperCollins*Publishers*

Some of these poems have been previously published in *The KGB Anthology*,
The Nation, *The New Republic*, *The New Yorker*, *The Paris Review*, *Poetry*,
Raritan, *Southwest Review*, *Theology Today*, *Threepenny Review*,
and *The Yale Review*.

HarperCollins books may be purchased for educational, business,
or sales promotional use. For information please write:
Special Markets Department, HarperCollins Publishers Inc.,
10 East 53rd Street, New York, NY 10022.

FIRST EDITION

Designed by Cynthia Krupat

Printed on acid-free paper

Library of Congress Cataloging-in-Publication Data

Galassi, Jonathan.
    North Street: poems/Jonathan Galassi.—1st ed.
      p. cm.
    ISBN 0–06–019540–1
    I. Title.
    PS3557.A387N67 2000   99-44294
    811'.54—dc21

00 01 02 03 04 BVG/HC 10 9 8 7 6 5 4 3 2 1

Again, for Susan

Contents

NORTH STREET

Water

When the water of forgetfulness
laps the boathouse dock and late light
floods the empty lake to bathe me,
where will you—lover sister
partner renewer—where will you be?

When the water of forgiveness
spirals and sucks
as it sinks too fast to the leaching field,
will you remember (what will you remember?),
reader healer redeemer sharer of mercy?

Water of memory   color of consolation
water of memory   taste of forgetfulness
touch of forgiveness   echo of acquiescence
color of consolation   water of memory

NORTH STREET

DITHYRAMBS

Knot

I want to get at the knot,
the white heat at the heart
of you, want to undo it,
the clot, the lock, the hot
rock, knock it back
so it opens to flood
and flow, for I know
great good will come of it.
Not that I get
all that high hitting home
(I can't, I don't, and I won't)
but up above where you sit
and the sun beats in your armpit,
I feel and love it,
inhale and swoon
with the smell, and I fell.
I flee, I lie, I try to fly,
but know it's not,
no, it's not on. What I've got
's not a lot of excitement,
not the loud
shout or tight shot,
but not nothing either,
my bright fuchsia lover;

together, whatever, I'm over-
spent, undersold,
blown, bent low
by your absolute predicate
weather, whether
you know it or not. . . .

Inside

There's dew on the ferns
and the goatsbeard that followed
so hard on the lilacs.
The copper beech's oxblood gown
is throwing shadows on the lawn,
the hummingbird is vectoring for nectar,
water collects in the pockmarked
granite, but inside the screen
dust motes hover over the stunned
miasma of the carpet
as young and strong you
come down lynxlike, liquid
muscle and tendon hipwise rolling
oiled and radiant, good as nude
but self-contained in skeins
your breast is straining,
warm breath mist like the filmy
curtains that lift off the hills.

Apparition, avatar of health,
broadcasting opulent
ease and ambition,
come, fill my shell
with your phenomenal
pheromone broth, make me over,

shape me, invert me, insert me
deep in your story.
Move my bones, sweep
my leaves, leavings, ash
for the time-capsule compact
bobbing awash in the chemical
bath of the future.
I'm a husk,
a flushed, hushed
ache for unlocking,
clueless bystander,
uninvited guest
at the wedding of sense and soul.

Flow

Down the path between the apples
through the maple grove of suicides
then left at the old wall
along the wire fence to the brook-
bank where narcissus noses
into skunk cabbage and hepatica:
Call me Apollo, crashing in the underbrush
with my arrows, my bow saw and clippers
out for your flash of white tail and alert
to hack me a path to your lair, to your cult's den,
crisscrossing the water with Phoebe again and again
as it elbows below us and runs
for the creek racks
strongest in springtime when everything's liquid,
tightroping over the rocks
in the plashing braid, hot on your sharp
scent and battling the mayflies
the black flies horseflies mosquitoes there under
the raspberry brambles and getting no nearer . . .

Or am I fleeing your coiling uncoiling
tentacular embrace
battered and scarred, am I seeing
your fabled face in the oily pools,
are these fern hairs sprouting at your knuckles

branchbones, little leaves halving
our limbs with leaves—are they yours or mine?
Your bloodhounds bay at the copper
creek, your velvet cape's aloft
in the chiaroscuro breeze, you're near, nearer,
hieing, heying, I'm falling, failing,
gashed, gutted, kneed-up,
muddy and galled—call me
Actaeon. . . .

Voice

Not your soothing shot-silk murmur
sweetest sound that replays in the pearl-
gray bedroom forever,
not the hoped-for words of conciliation
or the sigh, the line that melts with ruth
—Orbison Sinatra Smokey Stevie—
the adenoidal whine, the nasal
negative, the chirp, the coo, the undulant
murderous yell, not Daddy's intermittent
gravel-sweetness, chuckle and caress,
not the chirring brook and not
the winding, whingeing wind,
the tree frogs talking, the cicadas sawing,
not the striped straw sucking air
when the ice cream soda's history
or the traffic barreling down North Street,
incessant droning of the BQE,
not my own uneven breathing,
inner music, tissue of remembrance
—Madonna Judy Cher Aretha Callas—
not hard words, harsh laughter
heard unbroken or the silence after
leaving, not the rueful
tears, not sullen, sultry silences from too-full
lips; not silvered hair;

but the unstifled stillness at rock bottom
that wells up out of bile after defeat
to oil the water. Everything is over
and still it says, Get up,
start over.
What you have to do.
Begin.
Again.

Walk

Something's missing on Bald Mountain Road.

The climb is steep until you reach the pond
choking with waterlilies, goosedown snagged
in the rushes at the edges.
Then along the field under the maples,
flatness arrived at, till you fall a bit
as the hills appear in layers, colors,
previews of the big view at the end—
the landscape leaving, the horizon hurting,
sunset comes so suddenly up here.

What do the trees do when the wind is tame
in the mild airplane murmur, total
summer effulgence:
clutch of vine thicket, insect echo chamber,
virtual standstill?
They put out roots, go deep, get down,
dowse for water in the stony soil,
get mirrored in another element,
try for the red-hot
core where the bodies are buried.
No more outreach, floating trial pennants
to gauge the gale.

Everything's underground,
bent on the future—
no way but down . . .

I'm mourning something on Bald Mountain Road.

Renewer:

the milkweed has cropped up again
in the summer field barely two weeks after mowing.
The pears and the peaches are round on the boughs
and it's only begun: Are we reaping or sowing?

*

Manure makes the valley route sharper, enhances
the ride to the west where connectedness happens.
I run to my mate, to my muse, to my maker
aroused in the reek as the August dusk deepens.

*

Item: afternoon wasted regrouping,
revamping, redressing, repotting, replanting,
daydreaming, moonlighting, rabbiting, bickering,
scheming you everywhere, finding you wanting.

*

Churlish remaker, your absence can only
enhance my unshakable faith in enthrallment
as I stare at the shade on the long lawn at dusk
drink in hand and consider again what it all meant.

*

I should assault the impregnable tower,
bushwhack a pioneer route through the cornbrake;
but I'm off-kilter, petrified, ripe for rebuke:
a man's myth is evidently what he can't make.

*

The eclogue is over now, back to your book again,
ruiner, let the life be what it seems.
Beam me up soon on your dulcimer bandwidth
at home alone halving importunate dreams.

Swoon

Open-ended
like the swallow's
swoon, swift
swerve in the syrupy
light of high noon:

I was mended
when I returned your deft
serve to extended
arms, calm balm
in the jittering
dithyramb room:

arc subtended,
widening, rippling out
down into lithe
liquid moon-shadow,
into the gloom.

Darling, the föhn
is falling. Don't falter
or fail me now,
don't be offended:
close your eyes, hold

tight and swallow,
then follow me
down to the dune.

Thread

Heartworn happiness, fine line that winds
among the tapestry's old blacks and blues,
bright hair blazing in the theater,
red hair raving in the bar—as now
the little leaves shoot veils of gold
across the trees' bones, shroud of spring,
ghost of summer, shadblow snow, blood-
russet spoor spilled prodigal on last year's leaves . . .
When your yellows, greens, and yellow-greens,
your ochres and your umbers have evolved
nearly to hemlock blackness, cypress blackness,
when the woods are rife with soddenness
(unfolded ferns, skunk cabbage by the stream,
barberry by the trunks, and bitter
watercress inside the druid pool)
will your thin, still-glinting thread insist
to catch the eye in filigreed titrations
stitched along among beneath the branches,
in the branches where it lives all winter,
occulted fire, brief constant fleeting gold . . .

Bower

The squall is over, summer nearly peaked.
Now it's clear air, cool
nights, all downhill from here.
The peegee not the snowball tree
staggers so it almost
breaks from the weight of its blooms.
The field is shaggy: goldenrod, brown fern,
the treeline's shaggy,
starting to give up its green,
though the ewers of the money
plant are still pitching their nectar.

Summer's too much
and never enough
cornsilk and cornstalk
lily-choked pond water
weed-worried roadside
waiting for rain
waiting for rain
waiting
waiting
waiting for rain

and after the rain
when everything's crystal,

open, cool, purged
the peegee's blossoms
start to go brown or purple at the edges
depending on the soil
depending where you're standing
depending where you're going . . .

I'm going north to the purple
future, the strenuous
hard time,
south to the truth,
but the peegee stands its ground
and its paper flowers
will repeat its glistening bee-soaked
chorus in stiff-sheeted winter,
bower of abundance, undulant dooryard
harvest-star,
white willing rainbow
tree of tomorrow
and after tomorrow.

Differential

Over the stream the snowcrust
gleams with potential—
sun under acid sky
there but not here
like the differential
a turned page is
or a light
left off
or on
you here with me
or gone
my object hunger
strong where the sun is
ray-drenched
limitless, limb-
loosened, sated . . .

Oceans dogs and Arabs,
mountains cats and Jews—
which are you
which are we all
black/white
1/2
he/she   me/
you

now and then dead
or alive
on the digital
blade between
seen and unseen

SACKETT

STREET

View

Isabel, I have been pushing you
for more than half an hour on this playground
horse as high as it safely goes—
which isn't nearly high enough for you.
The rain is just holding off, or not quite just,
which means we're by ourselves in this place
that's usually thronged on a late-spring
Brooklyn Sunday afternoon
with fathers doing their weekend fathering
(some trying to doze, or sneak a look at the paper
between flights and falls and wars on the bars).
But the damp doesn't faze us: you adore your dangerous
horse, and the mournful Steve Reich sound its swinging
makes in its endless rise and fall
is the forever music of this moment.

I love the view I get from here,
not just you in your gaiety,
but the whole harbor: Wall Street, Governor's Island,
the Statue in her scaffolding, the halls of Ellis Island,
the spires and towers and bridges of Jersey.
The water today is corrugated cardboard,
just that gray, the same gray as the sky.
Four cargo ships are docked below us,
beyond the runners who keep passing

alone or in pairs, not seeming to notice the scene
or that they're part of it;
there are mysterious boxes—sidecars?—on one deck,
maybe twice my height, although the scale
is hard to tell from here (there are no people),
and rows of toy trucks and barrels on another.
At least three kinds of conveyances
are going about their business in the harbor.
The biggest are the yellow-orange
ferries for Staten Island: one has just pulled
into the copper-green housing that seems to lead
to the hell under Manhattan. The less frequent white
Coast Guard ferries for Governor's Island
seem to crisscross the others' path,
and the red-and-white Circle Line tour boats
look almost too small for what they do,
which is to trudge forever around the big island.
And somewhere out there, too,
are the ones for the Statue,
threading among the unscheduled barges and tugs,
sailboats, tankers, and liners.
All these Sunday conveyances on their regular errands
(not to mention the several machines in the sky)
plying their trade in one big, busy room!
Who could take in everything they've seen:
the smugglings, mutinies, battles, embraces,
fires and flotillas,
yet they all keep soldiering (sailoring) on, as if life were only
this slipping away from the dock and making off
to the destinations defined by their speed and capacity.

I say, hats off to their tenacity,
not to mention their color and verve,
that belie their gray surroundings.
Hats off to the jaunty parade they make of their work,
the Sunday painter's curlicues of smoke
twirling up from their stacks, the vestigial
life preservers on their blunted prows,
the proud way they progress in spite of their heft,
these old undaunted harbor dowagers.
Or maybe they're new like you and don't make do
but can only be what they feel.
Nothing stops you either, not choppy water,
silence, or solitude.
You forge ahead like them, your laughter flying
in the face of the uncertain weather and my mood.
Your life is motion,
you can't imagine falling or failing.
You keep on sailing while I push,
the swing sings, and a gentle rain
keeps not quite darkening the ground;
Sunday continues, and another ferry
leaves for another run around.

May

The backyard apple tree gets sad so soon,
takes on a used-up, feather-duster look
within a week.

The ivy's spring reconnaissance campaign
sends red feelers out and up and down
to find the sun.

Ivy from last summer clogs the pool,
brewing a loamy, wormy, tea-leaf mulch
soft to the touch

and rank with interface of rut and rot.
The month after the month they say is cruel
is and is not.

Snapshot

Who's that on the porch at Ephesus,
the thin one, with the sprouting shoulderblades
and the polo shirt piled on his head
to keep the poison Turkish sun away?

Who's that by the sand cliffs on Block Island,
standing with Giovanna, with Diana,
the maladroit one, pale and embryonic,
squinting, with the hair down in his face?

I can see your eye behind the camera,
the shape you give to things, your favorite sweater
draped on the chair. I hear the bells
of Recanati, I can even almost taste the joy,
the ouzo and the oktopodia. But who's the boy?

Youth,

       it falls through the fingers
like money we thought we had
and only the aftertaste lingers—
like salt, like water, like lead.
I spent mine being afraid.

I see it now in the tender
shadows that loom on the wall:
One is solemn and slender,
the other is wired and small.
Very soon they will be tall.

I hold them and nearly drown
in the pooled brightness there.
Almost—but the lightning's gone.
Now it lives in their wounding unreadable stare,
in their skin, on their lips, their bewildering hair,
in the terrible newness they are.

Bequest

Enormous changes have been in the offing
here where it is all right to be rich.
The future has been nailing shut its coffin
and handing out its heirlooms, each to each.

The lady pours her jewels on the bedsheet,
the wealth that she has called up from her vault.
Her trembling hand can barely lift the spreadsheet
as she assigns an emblem to each fault.

You get the sapphires of the piercing blue,
the deep fjords that were fired for drowning in,
garlanded with diamonds like snow;
my carbuncle is carnelian.

And no appeal's allowable in there;
this was the finding of the highest court.
No one ever claimed that life is fair;
what comes after is a rougher sport.

Ozone

The sun is sharp, the clouds are roiling,
and the snow is sweet
out here in the ozone
where realities compete.

The basalt streets are severed by
the avenues that freeze
the neon traffic's streaking rainbow
time-lapse energies.

One shivers on magnetic north,
another heading west
cuts off his trajectory
murderously fast—

each one hounded by a vision
instants apart and not again;
vectors verging on collision
where one man's poison is another's rain.

Flâneur

New York without him never is the same:
no late, long lunches at Il Giglio,
no phone tag, dog talk, aimless walks,
or lubricated nights to fuel
Roman invective, accurate and cruel:
our minute bleeding at its yellow roots
in lines as tailored as his Huntsman suits,
signs for the unsuspecting that they knew
a sole survivor of the Happy Few.

Who wears street clothes anymore? Who shoots
his cuffs, or stuffs his napkin in his collar?
Who pans for hours down Broadway, secret scholar
of glamours, powers, frauds, cupidities,
then cuts and swivels to his neon screen
to pin them down, *simplex munditiis*?
Man of qualities but not illusions,
who deals in them with savage sleight-of-hand,
who makes a virtue of a boutonnière
and stares the crowd down. . . . How did Baudelaire
define the dandy: setting sun,
Hercules on welfare, aristocracy of one,
seer in contacts who acknowledges
that love is time and money, and disdain
the last refuge of a man in pain. . . .

Freddy, New York is on the wane.
She needs a bleeder for her cankered heart,
a cold Cavafy for her evening.
The painted lady wants you home
from the fleshpots of your Rome
for a last finger of Old Rarity.
Tap in your million-dollar shoes,
put the old poses to the test:
Your nose will lead you where the shooting is
because they cost, because they are the best.

The Shock

I take the dusty yearbook off the shelf
and scan the fledgling, mostly white male faces:
a foreign country, but the aging self
created there is marbled with its traces.

But do the scrubbed looks in the photos show us
inklings of our later being here?
Are they the Ur-forms of us as we know us,
or sometimes are we shades of what we were?

Remember Eddie Baker's ears,
Alex Reti's slouch and pout,
Bruce Sloan's watery eyes and sort of slur,
and Peter Burns' myopic stare,
his slow, impassive Southern courtesy
intended to not quite conceal
he wasn't sure you were for real—

And the white-gold shock of Surfer Wallace's hair
swaying as he runs down the chapel aisle,
bright California rag he shakes with a smile,
shorter and neater than it will be in a year
but already a rowdy banner, a provocation:
his whip, his matador's cape, his topsail flapping—

who can forget the shock of hair
and the nonchalance that was probably largely fear
as he sprints to the rising surge of rhythmic clapping,
chased by his demons as far as he can get?

Nothing—accident, earthquake,
plague, or starvation—has erased it yet.

August

I can see you standing in the corn,
flashing a little if a little breeze
rifles the rows that waver toward the barn,
and everything your golden body is

is laid out in the fields, along the roads,
ripe for the gathering: so much of it
that more than half goes begging in the weeds
whose wretchedness of excess shames the fruit.

August: Another paean blares its message
into a sunstruck, far-from-waiting sky.
But tiny crimson fault lines etch the edges
where other energies will soon let fly.

Bud on Bud

The poet bends
over the kitchen table,
working her poem.
Her long brown neck
with its hair
wisps shines in the light.

She writes about the first
rose from the garden,
herald of summer,
there in a water glass.
She takes its measure,
makes it her own,
the way her words about leaves
enshrined them forever.
Then she draws roses
over her lines about roses.

They are as green and involute
as the bud she writes about—
bud on bud, unfolding
at the kitchen table.

Turning Forty

The barroom mirror lit up with our wives
has faded to a loaded-to-the-gills
Japanese subcompact, little lives
asleep behind us, heading for the hills

in utter darkness through invisible
countryside we know by heart by light;
but woods that are humane and hospitable
often turn eerie on a moonless night.

Our talk is quiet: the week's triumphs, failings,
gossip, memories—but largely fears.
In our brief repertoire of poses ailing's
primary, and more so with the years

now every step seems haunted by the future,
not only ours, but all that they will face:
a stricter world, with scarceness for a teacher,
bad air, bad water, no untrammeled space—

or so it seems to us, after the Fall,
but for the young the world is always new.
Maybe that's what dates us worst of all
and saves them: What we'll miss they never knew.

We're old enough now to be old enough,
to know what loss is—not just hair and breath;
each has eyeballed reality by now:
a rift, a failure, or a major death.

They landed on us; we were not consulted,
although our darkest yearnings aren't so deep.
Let's tick off the short wish list of adulthood:
sleep, honor, sleep, love, riches, sleep, and sleep . . .

and camaraderie, that warms the blood,
the mildest, most forgiving form of love.
In an uncertain world a certain good
is one who'll laugh off what you're leery of.

That's why we're out here, racing with the clock
through cold and darkness: so that, glass in hand,
we'll face our half-life, padded for the shock
by a few old souls who understand.

Now the odometer, uncompromising,
shows all its nines' tails hanging in the air.
Now an entire row of moons is rising,
rising, rising, risen—we are there:

Total Maturity. The trick is how
to amortize remorse, desire, and dread.
Eyes ahead, companions: Life is Now.
The serious years are opening ahead.

RAYOGRAMS

False Memory

The sky's broad Sanforized electric blue
shirt sit ever lightly on your back,
but always, always open at the neck
so that it makes a window on the skin
which is an image of the self within

whose emanation haloes every thing,
every chink and cranny where you live:
not just the burnished fall frame of the lake
(you on the rock wall, you in the canoe),
but with false memory's zealous fixative
offering its earnest you are you.

I have this power: I can conjure you,
I can put you here. But what I can't
do is find the buttonhole, the tear
that opens on the universe next door.
The dream is what it is, not what I want.

You haunt the dock the way the water snake
curls on the top step, drowsing in the sun,
waiting for you, because you are the one
he has to change his skin with to come back.

And there's no difference: present or away,
with me or against me, you are here.
The water's glint reflects you, go or stay.
Your negative gets printed everywhere.

Siren

In your think tank you're Olympia,
all languid length and skin and two red roses
budding in the suds; or you're unhappy, a
sea fury frozen in your fountain poses.
And then a fine rime settles on the water,
hides you almost, Susannah, soaped to gleaming,
but wise from birth to what the elders taught her,
that though the tongue be stone the spirit's scheming
heat and action, craves to be
swimmimg with you into infinity—
as on those evenings when I hear you run
your bath and put your hair up in a bun
and sigh, and sink into your second home,
and then you call me from the other room.

Girlhood

If your bearded friend
helps you catch the trout
barehanded
in the pool of the dream
and you carry it in his pail
barefoot
up the rocky stream
to the playhouse where he fries it in his pan;
if you snip the dill
for the carrots and then swim
until your lips are bluer than the lake
where will it take you?
Not anywhere as pure
and primal as these sunstruck days
sistered by starstruck nights.
Don't cloud the drowning
brightness of your eyes,
don't answer my asking look
with anything but the truth,
don't spill the fresh-picked
raspberries on the car seat
and stain your shirt with indelible blood.

Or spill them, darling.
How else will you know

the color of crushed time;
how else will you feel
what it is to change and remember,
to lose and absorb
this summer inside you,
xylem and phloem of your leafy future
already starting to spread its shade above us?

The Necklace

These little irises could be your eyes'
if they were twice as large and twice as dark,
but if I got inside them—can I find
the vein that is the tunnel to your heart?
I may be in there: I see signs of movement
under the silky shadow/luminescence;
is it feeling's fierce integument
or a more troubled, more elusive essence?
Your other eyes have locked me out sometimes
(they have good reason to) but not ignored
the guilty pleading boring out from mine
there are no words for, as there are no words
for what these lacquer seeds say. Irritation
brought them on, but patience made them pearls,
the same slow labor that piles years of pages up—
call it obsession, plodding, imitation,
pigheadedness, simplicity, devotion:
Out of the dented life burled nacre curls
until the final jewel locks rays and rages up.
Remember when you wear these little worlds.

The Man on the Raft

The man on the raft
is backlit, like the leaves
on the branches between us,
dark body edged
in gold at the shoulders,
and the hair on his arms,
if we could only
see it, is also gold
this time of day,
this time of year.
He has been sitting for hours
because the day
is not quite over
and he wants to watch it
go out quietly,
go out beautifully,
not like a light, like a day,
deepening, darkening
like summer skin.

The hour is backlit, finishing,
gilding what had to be.
The broken branch is beautiful
in afternoon, when colors
thicken on their way to fading.

Greens get velvet, moody,
slashed by birches. The water's
sapphire-colored,
bronze, or platinum,
and everything
is over and done with, all
that's left is the framing.
And the lapping on the stones,
the dry spume on the planks
are over, too:
Day's ending,
summer's ending;
only the love lives on,
the wound that won't heal.
Say good-bye to today's
remorse, tomorrow
is already half
over somewhere else.
And when he stands and stretches
and dives to swim to the dock,
the man's head
in the ebony light-
flecked water is only
a node on the rim of evening
where the gold
is starting to fade
into the pinks and reds
and purples of the dome.

*

The sun is setting: think
of what got added today,
the building, the mating and saving,
made things, layer on layer,
snow lying over ice,
and we trek across it, trying
to keep on the perilous crust.
And think of what leaches down
through the soil into the cistern
that gathers most of the rest:
the waste work, the hate, the hard deaths,
losses that don't get saved.
There are no permanent graves;
look at the stones, forgotten
names facedown in the grass.
Weather or rootwork felled them,
no matter their artful carving,
and all that's left is a pattern
of shadows on the ground,
the twigs and spume that jostle
next to the mossy rocks,
and the pool of light collecting
behind the invisible man
swimming in from the raft
in the white wake of the sun.

*

The places light is leaving
burn with the brightest fire,
maybe to show they are saving

their unfinished desire.
Or maybe the gold leaf
that edges the highest leaf
signals tomorrow's claim,
its claw, its offer of grief.

Clouds appear
out of nowhere, wearing
high romantic colors—
mauve, peach, lavender.
Clouds of glory: we
know something about them,
but they have nothing to tell us
about what's going to come.
Is this why late light is
so condensed and clear,
that this is its last chance
for some resemblance here?
Resemblance—what we stare
into the water for;
but daylight is the thing
that lets it be a mirror.
The man who has spent it all
on the raft tries, swimming back,
but now for him the water
is only flat and black.
A glint might be his reflection,
but there's no way to know.
Nothing left for him to do
but try again tomorrow.

Argument

Chaotic sun on asphalt camouflages
the order of the shadows that the trees
throw down in mulled, elliptical mirages:
wheels within wheels—I've had my share of these.

The clouds upstairs, too, seem to move by magic;
their wayward travels never look the same.
I can't see their wildness has a logic
and I don't know my wildness has a name.

A Compass for J. and C.

What's your sign? Who's your most
unforgettable character? Where
are you going? Why are you staring?
What have you lost?

Questions as profuse as the powderpuffs
over Mount Riga, or their shadows shifting
on the sides of the shaven heads to the east and southwest,
falling away down the valley into the cauldron,

for this is a place for seeing things whole,
from above, in the round, as if they were ours
to plow through and scatter, to study or sway with
and use up, or try to husband and comprehend.

North is Thinking, putting a glaze
on occurrences and now and then channeling them.
South is Feeling, where the body flows
and the heart follows, not unwillingly.

Intuition arrives from the East like morning,
and Sensation never sets but keeps leaving in waves,
impetuous, insatiable, impossible to predict,
driving us on, and it takes all the intuition,

thinking, and feeling inside us to hold it in place.
It's the whole show at first. Reasons
come later, after the marriage of thinking
and feeling, brokered by intuition.

But we're getting ahead of ourselves. Spin the wheel,
travelers; whatever it decides—
NE, SW, true W—our intuition tells us
your thinking and feeling together will be a sensation

—and it will take a lifetime to answer the questions.

Heedlessly

Sharer of our mountain bike,
Altezza, can't you tell
your heart drives this stop-
and-start agglomeration
of wheel-within-wheel that gets
stalled on the steep places, lets it
pull through somehow?

Wrinkles in the water were repeating
the quivering that visited your chin,
as I sat by you stony, helpless, waiting
for a new breeze to bring us better weather.

The silence now is like my silence then:
it's the bagged wind begging for a breather,
the stunned day not knowing what to say
to the questions that you send its way.

I'm out in my pith helmet on the prowl
for liveliness I can pass off in words,
but if I hear it rustling in the weeds
it's gone before I bend down with my bowl.

So, if the sounds are unforthcoming,
it's that the few I latched onto

struck me as false, or unbecoming,
or for show,

though your water name is drumming
in the alcaics the canoe
writes as it knocks on the rocks,
and your shape and feel can mold me
more wholly than the wind could ever do.

I told you, darling: Words aren't fuel,
looks aren't, offers, deeds are only
intimations of tomorrow's motion
that bends to you, implores you:

Must we spend
our little store of graces needlessly,
when it's apparent every living notion
begs and borrows from you and adores you
and imitates your sorrows
heedlessly?

Rayogram

Your negative gets printed everywhere,
not only on the water fields that stay
put although the wind gets busy here,
trying to beat the August haze away

until another slow breeze lobs it back—
but in the dream, too, where you are the one
caught in a slow bake, drowsing in the sun
(but otherwise not very like the snake).

The dream is what it is, not what I want,
I told you; all its props come from next door,
the world inside the tear-
drop, nothing more. I've tried but I can't
change it; if I conjure you

or banish you, you're you:
memory, emanation, fixative,
red water, pitch dark sky, and pale canoe
arriving from the far end of the lake
where the unseen fabled others live
and the bug light frazzles everything.

Here is an image of the self within:
decked out in warpaint brighter than your skin,

immersed in the white lake up to your neck
and kicking: you, absorbing on your back
the sky's broad Sanforized electric blue.

HARVEST

The Canaan Rainbow

The greatest thing I've ever seen
was the Canaan rainbow, promising
what? We'd stopped for dinner in the rain,
but suddenly the sun was out again
and there above the parking lot
bands of color filled the August sky
as wide as four-lane highways.
You had to wonder what had happened there
to make for such ionic air
and so much future over everything.

We stood awhile inside the humming cool,
staring. And then we left (can you believe it?).
The girls were cranky, it was time for bed,
Sunday evening was coming down.
I tried to keep it in the rearview mirror,
but once we'd made the curve on 44
our rainbow disappeared behind the hills.

That was the greatest thing I've ever seen,
and if I had it all to do again
(I know I won't; it doesn't work that way),
I'd stand my ground as long as there was daylight,
taking in the colors and their curves
until I couldn't tell them from the night.

I'd stay and let the magnet work its magic,
pulling every failing out of me
until the faucets of my eyes had opened,
my blood was pulling air, and I was free.

Apaquogue Elegy

FOR C. S. AND W. M.

September brightness sharpens everything
even when the windshield isn't clear,
and the backlot ragweed is conspiring
to flaunt the leveled floodtide of the year
before it hunkers down and loses scope
the way an old man has to. We were rich, too,
blowzy and effervescent and profuse
with future, till we lost it.
That's the here-and-now: always the same,
a blank slate without predetermined rules;
and color is collusion, just a game,
the way the cosmos and cleome stand
bald in the stationary light,
and the afternoon is wide and tight,
crystalline, invigorated, clean.

The fields were realer once, when these were farms
and the cornrows ran out to the sea.
Then the trees were landmarks
and the house stood up against the clouds,
making the sky seem taller.
Now everything's boxed-in except the sky.
The fields are mazes and the hedges hide
windowpane-and-shingle palaces,
overnight sod, mail-order border gardens.

Graveyard or green grid, the city
always only replicates itself.
Nature and nurture: big imbroglios
at the seams, where the underbrush
overwhelms everything every summer.
We went gathering
the purple and aquamarine berries and found
the soon-to-be-broken bittersweet still whole
where the asphalt starts to buckle,
where the beach roses are and the sand slides in
when the wind gives the little rise its razor cut.
Everything will bow down soon enough,
but now it's simple sun and shade and pride—
and the pewter sheet beyond the dunes,
the big water that goes everywhere.

*

Keep up the good work:
Cut back the climbing roses on the porch,
prune the box by the driveway and the hydrangeas,
pile the porch chair cushions in the dining room
by the bikes. Then wander
in the old inn, the unbelievable island.
Downstairs is always cool: blue rooms
swimming underwater in the salt
solution of Before;
blackened tennis trophies, vases,
furniture whose Florentine veneers
are cracked from lives of salt and damp,

chintz slipcovers from 1954,
foxed prints, old maps, old faces
steeping in the tea of memory.
Upstairs is golden: stippled walls,
curtains horizontal in the breeze
by the hall phone with its table and chair.
Rummage in the half-empty
third-floor bedrooms: stacked
hatboxes, old De Pinna dinner suits, forgettable
books, their twenty-year-old author photos'
painful, childish chic. . . . And where were you?
Just look in the shoebox of snapshots;
we're history, like everything around us—
except the others, who will bury you
not having worn bell-bottoms,
Greek shirts, hip-high patent leather boots,
or endless hair. But who's to say
the sleep was deeper then,
the talk more exuberant, the love
less tested? Maybe now,
or then, in the aftermath, is when
to be here. The room is half as long
as the house, its scrubbed white
floorboards are a quarterdeck.
You feel a little queasy after dinner,
and when you half wake in the gray half-
light it almost seems
the old brass bed is floating out to sea.

*

The after-sunset lounging on the sand,
unhemmed backlit moments: tousled hair
and martinis in a Mason jar,
toasts lifted on the cusp of night,
midair leaps into oncoming lights
and fiery kites nose-diving into the dark
are over. Now the trees' old ladies' hands
salaam the sky, and bittersweet
makes bonfires at the crossroads. Broken bits
of leaves are lined in rows across the lawns
and underfoot the witches' brew is steeping:
rainwater, twigs, mud, rust.
Now the land is skeletal it's much closer
to showing its hand; man's self-made monuments
snarl cheek by jowl, vying for dominance.
So much grandeur in such little space
makes everything petty—
except the stern old upright
house, arms akimbo,
staring across at its neighbor the angry water.
The squash is rotten, the fields are stubble,
the final apple's speckled on the branch.
It's gone again, illusion of accrual;
winter's birds are boiling up above.

*

The future is out on the lawn
playing tag in bright clothes under clouds
driving east like floes in a breaking stream.

Winter was here, but you missed it. Now evaporating
dew and sweet dog shit snap in the air like laundry
and the green in everything is yellow.
Remember the potato smell of the fields
when they grew potatoes? Remember watching
the Canada geese, flock after flock
pushing south as high as the planes,
and every time we looked up there were more,
and we loved fall more than before?
That was for us—but what will they remember,
what's been printed on the hidden map,
the silent codebook that gets handed on?
What do they make of the house,
the field, the sky, and the sea?
They've known them as a womb,
their own but not their own,
felt but not understood
or understood but unknown.
And what does it make of them,
what has it made of us,
trekking through the old rooms
where the paint is cracking again,
shuffling through the old books
like tourists who missed the bus?

The air inside gets filled
with light that is silvered with dust,
the mica glints as it tumbles
sifting slowly down.
The future is out on the lawn

ignoring us as it fixes
the indelible yellow-greens
of the then that will be then—
if the privet holds back the roaring
tiger-chase beyond,
if you smoke the bees from the chimney,
and the roof and foundation stay sound
of the old Pandora's box,
the boa that wants your last breath,
but has already turned its ravening eye
on the new prey out on the lawn
caught up in the ongoing game
in the blustery spring sun.

North of Childhood

FOR B.

Somewhere ahead I see you
watching something out your window,
what I don't know. You're tall,
not on your tiptoes, green,
no longer yellow,
no longer little, little one,
but the changeless changing
seasons are still with us.
Summer's back,
so beautiful it always reeks of ending,
and now its breeze is stirring
in your room commanding the lawn,
trying to wake you to say the day is wasting,
but you're north of childhood now and out of here,
and I've gone south.

Keepsake

Snatched from the lacquer waters of *L'anguilla*,
brass flash, brash flask of fleshtone gleaming in
the gloaming of the cold Vulcanic grotto,
rosary of word-pearls, open little book
emblazoned with a few fresh names for fire—
iris, rainbow, whiplash, arrow, siren,
sister—icons snaking in a kickline
that circles something far more sinuous,
like the flame that feints around desire.

Light means conflagration when the heat's
not locked up in the essence of a thing;
these matches will not strike because their blaze
is burning inward—catch it if you can:
today's trouvée, tomorrow's talisman.

Song Before

FOR M. AND R.

September happens.
After the overwhelmed
sown spring and blazoned
summer comes the calm:
tawny, human,
bearing, bodied;
time of fullness,
high point, still point,
time of alignment,
time of reward,
when the striving abates
and the year settles back
to enjoy what it is.
Follow its example
now, while the sated
sun still rains over nodding
loosestrife and goldenrod,
wonderful weeds of the hold-
over hour before,
today, not tomorrow.
See yourselves poised
as you crest at
the current's brim,
bask in the lull,
the hush,

the breath held back
until not now but tomorrow
two full streams
join in a fuller
river that overflows
to flood the alluvial
plain with the water
it needs to bring the new season,
and the getting
and spending begin again.

Harvest

Loved one, it has been my privilege
to calculate your sightings, near and far,
to swim in the wide wake of your effulgence
and watch you flare
in anger and arousal everywhere.

And on the windy afternoon of which I speak
burrs on my socks that stick and prick
unshakable as memories were clinging,
for I was running interference with
the Lilliputian pickers raiding the dwarf trees
while the ruddy sun, your other lover, was with you,
hurtling toward the clarifying west;
and you were there, too, laughing with the rest,
head tilted at that angle where you catch
the other, higher frequency you hear.

And strewn across the low fields by the sea,
boulders that had bounced on landing
burned as if to mock us two,
single or paired across the melted stubble,
some enormous, some mere rubble,
steaming coals, alive as anything
—except the careening nugget who thinks he owns you,
his influence so evidently flowing

from face to face across the crowd
arrayed in purple turtle fur and Lycra.

Then I was with him, and he let me see
our small careers: the gash and gleam,
the eddy, the crash and burn, the writhing quiet,
and it was very clear:
Loving isn't oneness, but aloneness.
The other stands out sharp up there;
each wears a sweater her own color,
no two the same.

Which is why just then, while you were all out
looking for the right one to bring home,
some emblem of achievement to get us to winter,
I kept to my bag of apples by the haycart,
though the day was far too full and carried no message,
no field disturbance, no slightest reason to doubt you,
and the need in me burned as it does in pure imitation,
still I stood there alone in the pumpkins without you.

Happenings

Forgiveness happens. Every now and then
the Canaan rainbow fills the valley up.
Hailstorms shatter August. Power fails.
A neighbor moves, or dies. A window falls.

Sun cuts through haze, and days are slowly shorter;
the road is dappled under the old tree;
the high wind stops its sanding: sudden silence;
a screen door slams; a guilty man goes free.

Turning Fifty

CHARM FOR C. H. H.

Unending afternoons are ancient history
when no blade stirred, an hour was half a week;
yet the scent of grass still holds its mystery,
now you're dealing close to a full deck.

Wife won, house built, new generation launched
(and, much to your credit, still no dog),
with wondrous works and days, all numbered, catalogued
for the bronze Domesday Book you may not want
to hammer into being in your den.

This is a charm for then, for while you wait
to paint its pages with distressed gold leaf,
or for unrelenting evenings when
you let the fire burn low and contemplate
that great unfinished work of art, your life.

Thank You

for everything I feel,
the inner whirlwind and the chill,
the hectic emptiness, the flare,
the hunger,
the anger.
Thank you for being the catalyst, thank you
for being thin air.

Thanks for the danger, the current that powers
straight up my arm to my chest from my finger,
thank you for letting me loiter and linger
anywhere near you, sing with the radio
driving down Broadway, being a hazard.
Thank you for hope,
for the pickerel smile,
thanks for the hair in the face and the laughter,
the long chase, the anguish before
and the dogginess after.

All of a sudden I woke and my pale face
confronted a sun,
my fingers were winnowing silver-streaked
paydirt, and you were the one.

The distance is orange,
your ominous presence is black.
My goal is to wreathe you in pillows
and worship you splayed on your back.

*(If I were stronger
or it lasted longer)*

The orchestra's tuned
and the feet are inured for the walk on the coals.
Your kerchief is there on the brush pile,
your smile fires the on-and-off gleam on the shoals.

Blind though you be to your manifestations
there on the map
they are the day- and the moonlight,
the headlight, the goal and the trap,
the handcuff, the blindfold,
the davening head and the prayer. . . .

Reader, the future is fuchsia,
I told you. Use it or lose it now,
strut in your insolent newspaper hat.
Thanks for the ague, the access,
the gnawing, the knowing,
the being and being here; thank you, dear.
Thank you for that.

Hymn

Will I meet you in the heaven
that I don't believe in, where
each of us is given
and forgiven our life here,

granted the fulfillment
of original desire,
forgiven the consumption
of ourselves in the world's fire?

In my dream I'm waking
in an unmown field, alone,
and everything is glistening
because the rain has gone.

I can hear the high weeds bending.
They are letting someone pass.
Is it you? I see us heading
to the same place on the grass.

Will we travel through each other
or reconstitute as one?
Will each truly see the other,
be the other in this sun?

I know what I have dreamed of
that my hasty heart has wrecked:
the paradise where parallel
intentions intersect,

the otherwhere I live for—
can it be the same for you?
It's against the laws of physics
and metaphysics, too.

But in the dream I'm dreaming
neither interferes.
Your defenseless eyes are searching,
I am open, and in tears.

There's no motion, no commotion,
only birdsong breaking through.
In the world I don't believe in
nothing's keeping me from you.

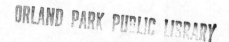